The Next Generation Science Standards (NGSS) are reproduced with permission from the Department of Education.

Written by Jake Hunter, Beth Hunter and Aysha Imtiaz

Illustrated by Bella Hunter

The Parts That Make Things: Noor's Magic Tiles

Student Edition

ISBN 978-1-952346-44-6

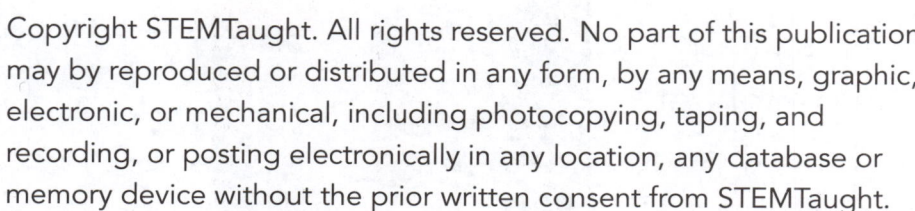

STEMTaught® Grade 2
Next Generation Science

Matter and Its Interactions 2-PS1-3:
Make observations to construct an evidence-based account of how an object made of a small set of pieces can be disassembled and made into a new object.

Wheee! I can fly!

Colorful Mosaics in Mexico

Once a year, in a small mountain town in Mexico, the streets come alive with color and the air is filled with music. The people of the town spend many hours working on beautiful street mosaics made from rice,

flour, sawdust, flower petals and colored sand. A mosaic is a picture made from smaller pieces.

Next, the town celebrates as a grand parade travels through the town while stepping on all the beautiful patterns.

When the parade is over, the children of the town get their chance to play and race over the mosaics.

Finally, it's time for everyone to clean up after the festivities.

Think, Pair, Share!

What are the designs on the street made from? What are those materials usually used for?

Lesson Anchor

Make your own mosaic using tiles

You can use these paper tiles to create your own mosaic! By putting these small pieces together, you can make a larger work of art! Many different designs can be created using the same simple pieces. What design will you make?

Step 1: Cut out your tiles.

Step 2: Arrange them to make a fun picture. Color them.

Step 3: Glue your tiles to a piece of paper to make your mosaic.

This student made a fun mosaic dinosaur!

Explore

Attention Getter

You will be surprised to see how many beautiful designs you and your classmates can make. You can make diagonal lines, flowers and even diamonds.

Cut out your tiles on dotted lines

MY MOSAIC

Cut out your tiles
on dotted lines ✂

Parents,

Your STEMTaught student has learned that many things are made of smaller pieces. Beautiful designs and artwork can be made from small pieces such as mosaic tiles. Please take time to create more mosaic designs at home with your child and ask them what they have been learning with STEMTaught.

Parent/child homework activity: Make a mosaic.

All you will need is paper, scissors, crayons and glue.

Step 1: Color your tiles. It does not matter how you color them.

Step 2: Cut out your tiles and arrange them to create your pattern! Then, glue your tiles to a piece of paper. You can even color the background to enhance your mosaic.

Think about things that you see and use everyday to answer the question.

Explain the phenomenon:

What types of things can be made from smaller pieces?

_____

_____

_____

_____

Draw a picture of something made from smaller pieces.

Trash can be terrific!

Little things can be used to create something big, beautiful and amazing! Different materials are useful for different purposes, but it's not always necessary to use the same things in the same old ways. This sculpture of a wasp is made from many small pieces of trash.

This wasp is made of junk pieces of metal.   *Artist: JK Brown*

Can you find it?

Find and label these items in the wasp sculpture above.

| mesh | drill bit | chain and sprocket |

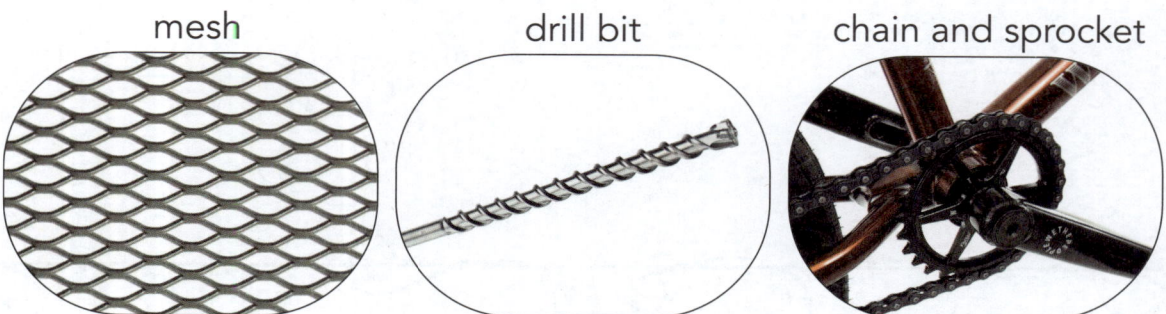

A welder is someone who melts metal pieces to join them together. Some people throw away their broken things because they don't see any value in them. The welder who made these sculptures collects things that other people call junk. He uses bent forks, rusty tools, and even scrap car parts to make his amazing sculptures.

Artist: JK Brown

Can you find it?

 Find and label these items in the frog sculptures above.

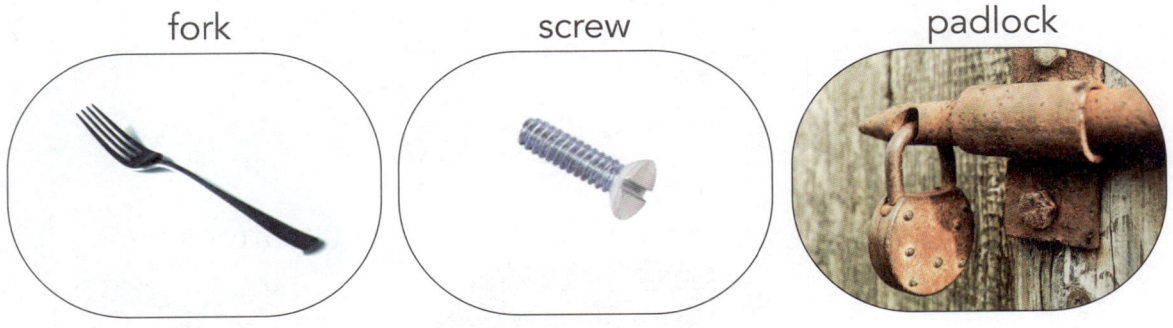

fork   screw   padlock

 Think, Pair, Share!

What other things would you use to make a metal sculpture?

Many things are made from smaller pieces

Many things can be made from a small set of pieces. We just need to be creative and see the beauty in everything to put those pieces together in just the right way.

metal file   door hinges   butter knives

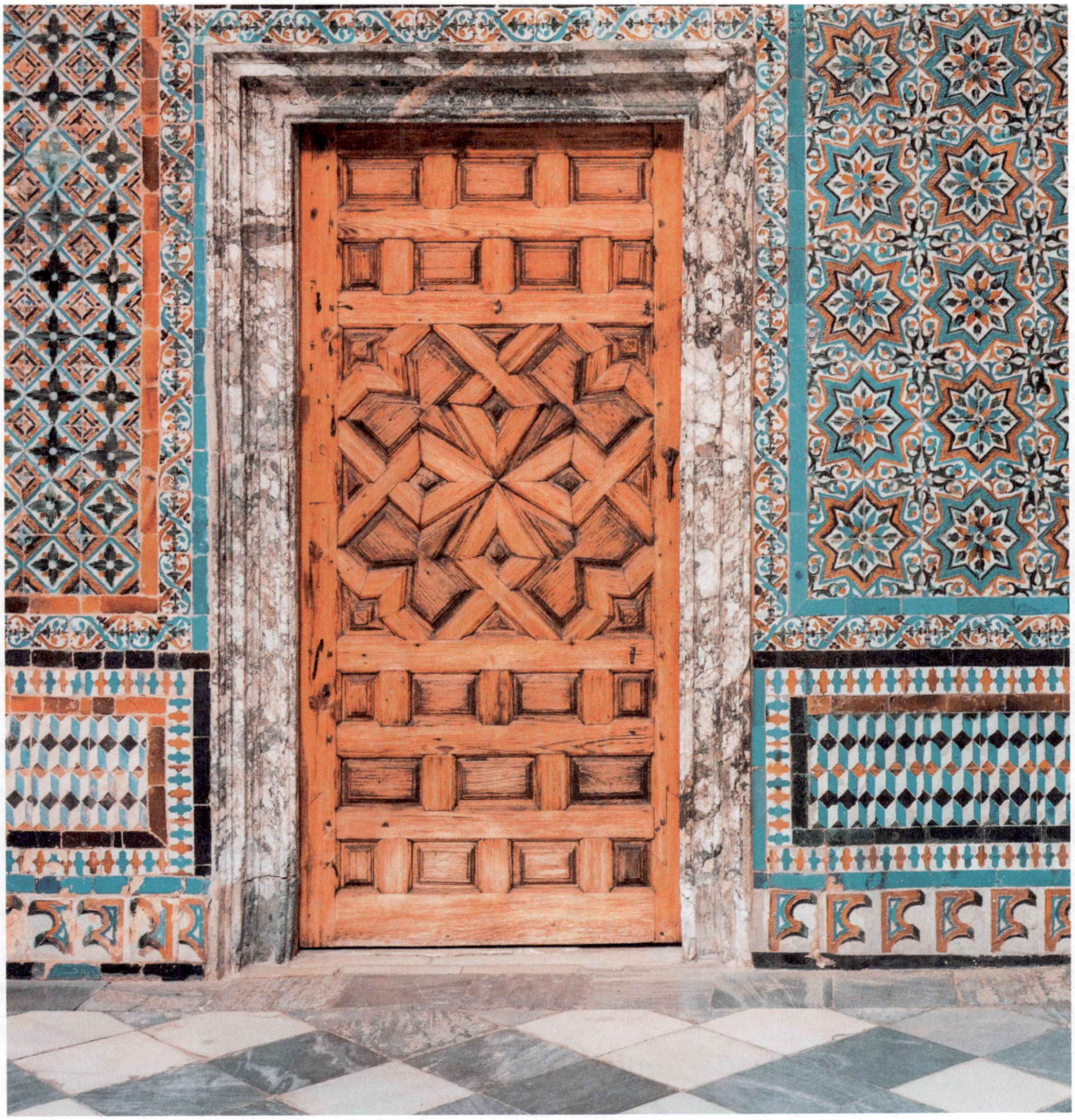

Blocks are really wonderful! They can be used to make so many different things. Can you see the small parts making something big here? The door, the floor, and the wall are all made from many small pieces.

 **Think, Pair, Share!**

What shapes, sizes, and colors are the blocks that make the door, the floor, and the wall?

Stone blocks come in many shapes

Blocks are really wonderful! They can be used to make so many different things. Many man-made structures are made of stone blocks. Look at these pictures. Can you see the small parts making something big?

Castle of the Knights of the Templar, Spain (built 800 years ago)

Knights in shining armor protected this medieval castle.

What are the sizes, shapes and arrangements of the blocks that make this structure?

_____

_____

_____

_____

Photo credit: Athinaios

Tumulus of Bougon, France (built 7,000 years ago)

Stone age people built this burial site more than 7,000 years ago.

Think, Pair, Share!

What are the sizes, shapes, and arrangements of the blocks that make this stone structure?

Anasazi Ruin, "River House,"
Arizona (built 1,500 years ago)

The Anasazi people built this cliff dwelling on the ledges of giant sandstone mountains.

 Think, Pair, Share!

What are the sizes, shapes, and arrangements of the blocks that make this stone structure?

*Pyramid of the Sun, Mexico
(built 2,100 years ago)*

The ancient people of Mexico built this pyramid by making a giant mound of dirt and then covering it with rocks. This is the third largest pyramid in the world!

 Think, Pair, Share!

What are the sizes, shapes, and arrangements of the blocks that make this stone structure?

_____

_____

_____

_____

_____

Make an animal with building barbs

You can make a lot of different things using the same types of pieces. Try it for yourself!

Use building barbs to create an animal of your own! It doesn't have to be a real animal, you can come up with your very own special and new animal if you wish.

Use scissors to cut your straws.

This tiny dragonfly was made using building barbs.

My Special Animal

Although there are only a few different types of building barb pieces, you can model just about any animal.

Describe the size, shape and arrangement of your parts.

_____

_____

_____

_____

Draw what you made.

Explore

Solidify
Understanding

Basic electronic parts make many things

What do a rocket ship and a microwave have in common? A lot more than you would think! Engineers create basic electronic parts and design creative ways to put the parts together to do different things. Clocks, lights, cameras, microwaves and even rocket ships have similar electronic parts in them.

Here is a close-up of a circuit board.

These students are taking apart a broken telephone to see what parts are inside.

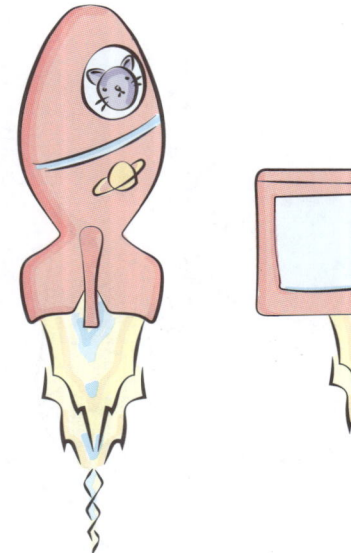

What do a rocket ship and your microwave have in common?

Real answer: They both have many of the same basic electronic parts in them.

Joke: They both can fly! Except for the microwave!

Have you ever looked inside an electronic device to see what makes it work? How does a clock keep time? How does a cell phone send your voice across the world? Each piece in an electronic device has a purpose. When they are arranged differently, they do very different things.

Resistor

I stop part of the flow of electricity in a circuit.

Capacitor

I store electricity, and then I release it in strong bursts.

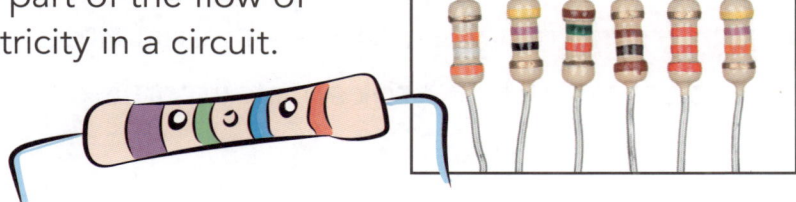

Transistor

I am a switch that turns on and off. Computers use me to store memory.

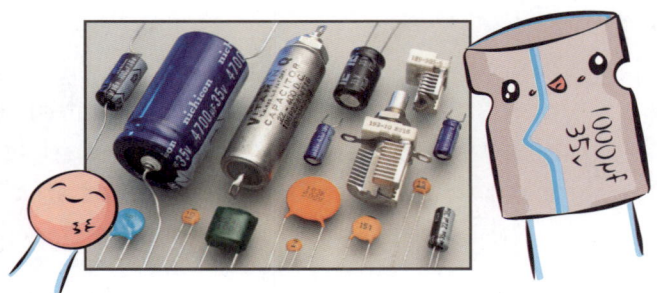

Diode

I make electricity flow in only one direction.

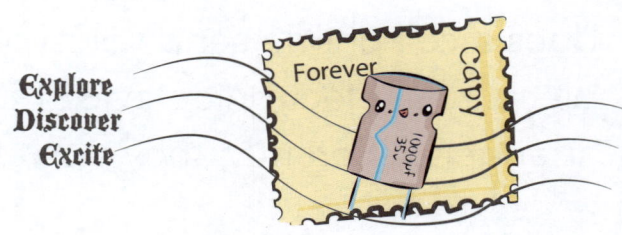

Parents,

Your STEMTaught student learned that basic electronic components can be put together in different ways to make a variety of electronic devices. Please spend time with your child to take apart an old or broken electronic device.

Parent/child homework activity: Take apart a small electronic device

You will need an old or broken electronic device to take apart. If you can't find one, thrift stores often have broken devices that they will give you for free. You will need some small screwdrivers to get inside the device. Please take apart a small device such as a broken telephone, alarm clock, keyboard, or hair dryer.

Caution: Do not take apart a large device such as a microwave or TV because large devices often have powerful capacitors that store voltage that can hurt you. **Make sure whatever device you take apart is not plugged in.**

Try to identify the parts on the backside of this page: resistors, capacitors, transistors, and diodes. You may also look for other interesting things such as magnets in speakers, LED lights, motors, and microchips.

The Parts That Make Things

I'm very important, although I am small
Join many of us together to make something tall
Building a pillow fort? Constructing a wall?
Smaller pieces are part of it all.

Arranging, re-arranging and moving around
Building down from the top or up from the ground
Whatever direction, wherever you go
I'm just a small part of something larger, you know.

Take me apart to make something new
Use many of us or just a few
Because the smallest parts are the special-est you see
Next time you look at something large, you'll notice me.

Can you find it?

- a spoon handle
- a wrench head
- a spring
- the head of a thumb tack
- butter knives

Artist: JK Brown

TANGRAM TILES

Some beautiful designs are made using Tangram tiles. Tangram puzzles were invented in China more than 700 years ago. The ancient Chinese called them Pinyin tiles. Designs made with Tangram tiles use seven small pieces. They can be put together in many different ways.

To solve the **BLUE** puzzles you can place your Tangram tiles directly on the pages of the book. Try it here!

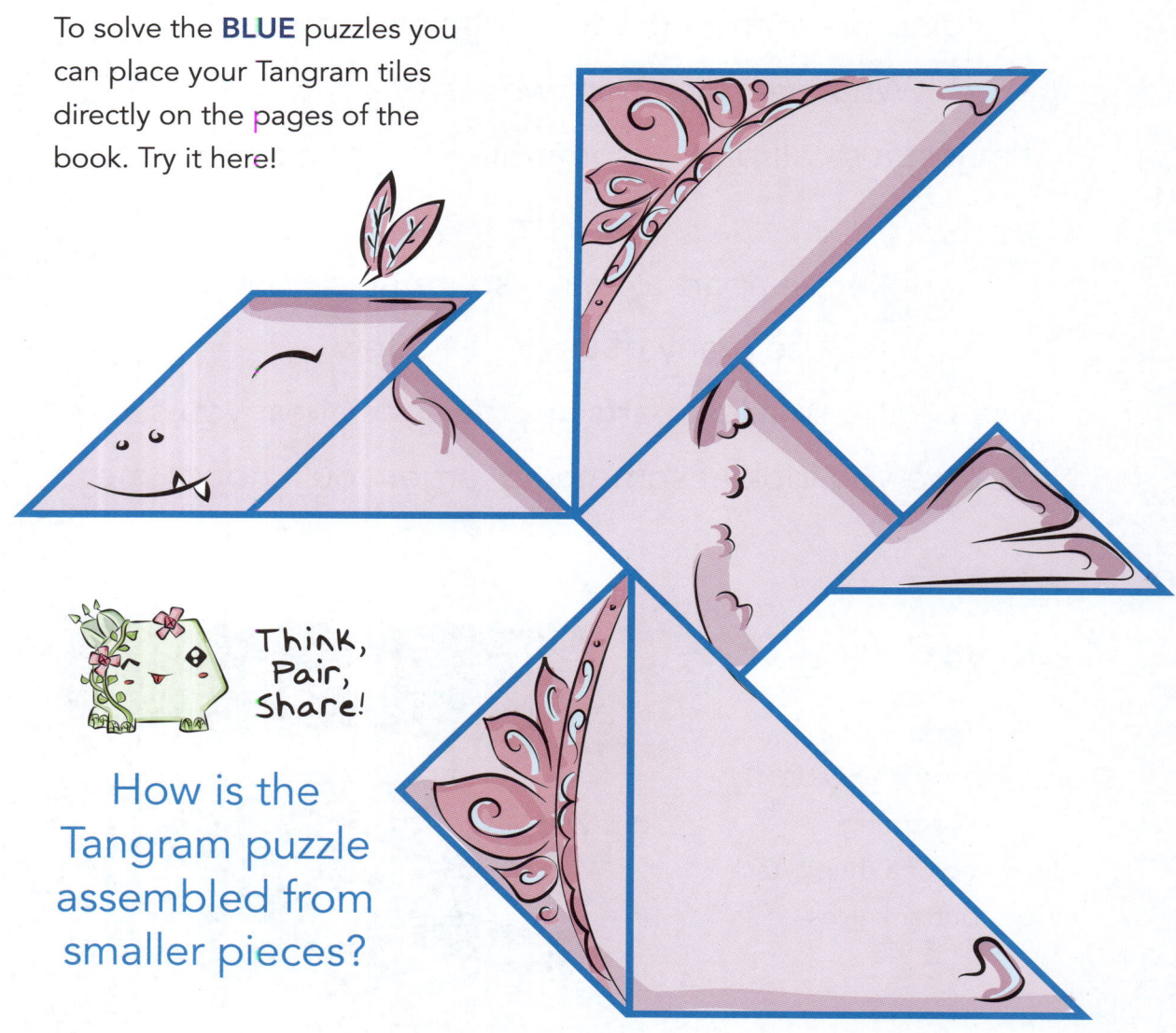

Think, Pair, Share!

How is the Tangram puzzle assembled from smaller pieces?

24

Cut out your Tangram tiles

Cut out these tiles to try making your own creations. Many designs can be made using the same seven pieces.

Cut on the dotted line.

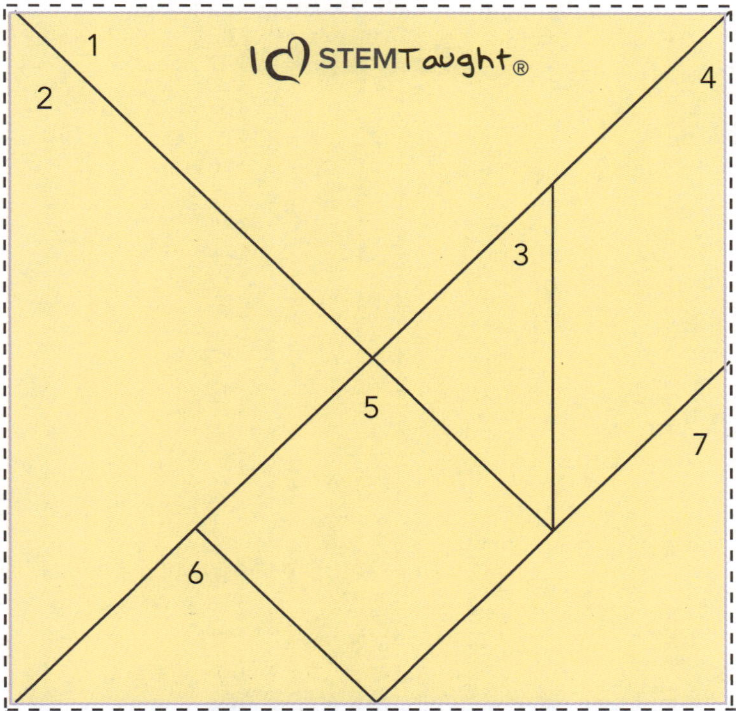
1
I ♡ STEMTaught®
2
4
3
5
7
6

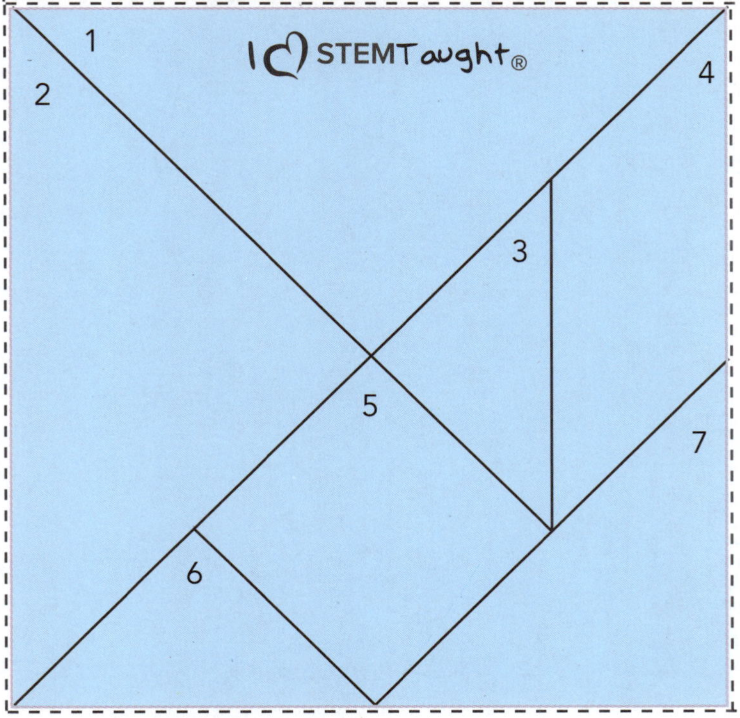
1
I ♡ STEMTaught®
2
4
3
5
7
6

1. Cut out the paper tiles.

2. Use your tiles to solve the puzzles.

Cut out these Tangram tiles.

Wheee!
I can fly!

Pterodactyls and velociraptors are extinct creatures that roamed Earth more than 200 million years ago. Try making a velociraptor from your Tangram tiles.

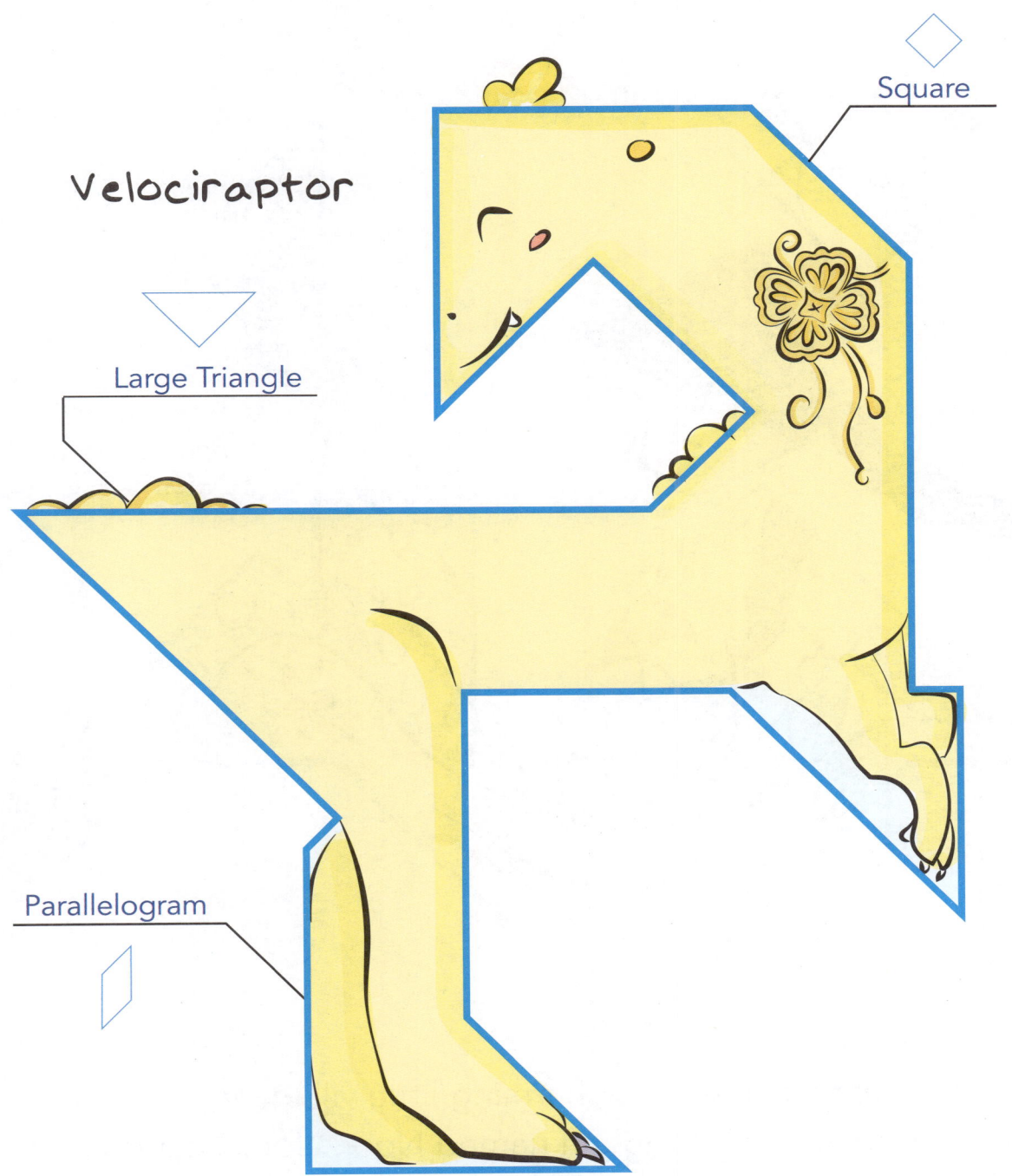

Velociraptor

Square

Large Triangle

Parallelogram

NOOR'S MAGIC TILES

Place your tiles here to make Noor.

Once upon a time, in a charming little village in Kashmir, there lived a young girl named Noor. Noor's name means 'light,' like the light that goes on in your mind when you have an awesome idea.

Noor's mother was beautiful. Noor thought her mother's face glowed like the moon.

However, Noor's life wasn't that bright lately. Times were hard in Kashmir. Her father couldn't find work. They rarely had milk, cheese or yogurt to eat, and even when they did, Noor's mother gave everything to the children.

Soon, things became even worse. In the middle of winter, the family ran out of food! They ate their last meal sadly.

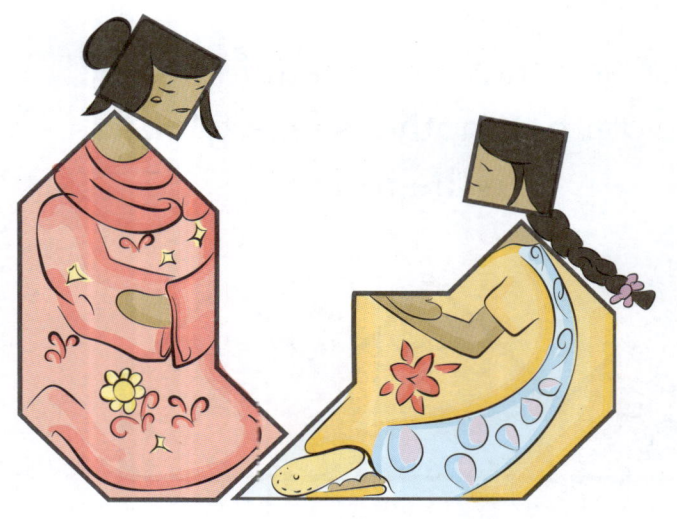

The next day, at supper time, Noor's mother came into her room. "Beti (daughter)" she said softly, "I am so sorry my dear. I have no supper for you tonight."

Noor was smart, brave and kind. She had a brilliant idea! She knew exactly what she had to do. When she had been born, her aunts and uncles had given her some gold coins. It was Noor's very tiny fortune, and she had been saving it her whole life.

Noor brought the pouch to her mother.

Place your tiles here to make the shape of Noor.

She said, "I want to use my fortune to help buy food."

Noor's mother had never wanted to ask her daughter for those coins because they were Noor's—but grateful for Noor's help, mother wanted Noor to choose her favorite foods to buy at the marketplace.

The next day, Noor set off for the marketplace. She knew her fortune was tiny, and it probably wouldn't get them much, but it would be a start.

As she walked, she dreamt of the food she would buy. Sunny yellow omelets appeared in her mind. She could almost hear the sizzling of eggs being cooked in homemade butter.

Lost in her daydreams, she barely noticed when a little boy, around her age, called out to her. "Behna (Sister)!" he said. In Kashmir, everybody called each other brother and sister.

"Yes?" Noor replied.

"Come closer," he said, "I have something to show you."

His fist was closed around something. When she bent in closer to get a better look, she saw that he held some softly glowing tiles with beautiful patterns on them.

The tiles were amazing! "What are these?" she asked, in wonder. The little boy explained that these were magic tiles. Whatever she made with them would come to life! Noor could barely believe it.

Noor was captivated by the tiles. She handed over her entire small fortune and got all three of the drawstring bags in return. Each bag had seven small tiles in it, which was enough to create one small mosaic each.

When she arrived home, her family expected Noor to have food, but they only saw the bags. When Noor opened the bags, it was not gold coins, but tiles which tumbled out. Noor's parents were very disappointed in her.

"You lost your small fortune," her mother said sadly.

Noor felt very ashamed of herself. She wished she had gotten food after all. 'The little boy must have tricked me,' she thought.

Before Noor went to bed, she set the useless bags of tiles in her younger brother Rayyan's room for him to play with.

Noor woke to the sound of Rayyan screaming.

"Sister! There's something outside my room. I could hear it ROAR."

When she looked outside his room, what she saw was truly amazing.

Standing there was a brilliantly colored and patterned, living, breathing dinosaur! Astounded, Noor realized what had happened.

Rayyan and Noor played with their dinosaur all day. They named her 'Umeed,' which means hope. Umeed stretched her neck to eat the leaves from the tops of pear trees.

As she ate, she knocked pears to the ground which Noor and her family hadn't noticed before. They ate the pears for dinner and weren't hungry that night.

Noor knew what she had to do now. She would use the tiles to create something that would make her family brilliantly happy for a brilliantly long time. She thought and she thought, and then, it came to her like a light that switches on when you have an awesome idea! Finally, Noor knew what she would make!

Nine months later ...

Ma's face is shining like the moon again. And there are no grumbly, hungry tummy sounds in Noor's home now. Instead, Noor hears the happy cluck-cluck sound of her magic chicken, Coco, and the bleating of her magic milk goat, Pogo. Ma makes many omelets using Coco's eggs, followed by a nice, tall glass of milk from Pogo. And Umeed? Well, most of all, she loves her joint owners, Noor and Rayyan, and ...

... lately, she has been carefully tending
to her gigantic purple egg!

Think, Pair, Share!

What would you make if you had three sets of magic tiles?

Use one set of Tangram tiles to create something of your own.

What is it? _____

Trace and decorate your creation here.

My amazing Tangram tile creation.

My Special Creations

What makes your creation special?

_____

_____

_____

_____

_____

_____

_____

_____

Puzzle Solutions

Play Sugar Glaze!

What you will do:

1. Cut out the game piece tiles.

2. Place the tiles face down in a stack.

3. Draw a card and place it in the playing area.

4. Take turns drawing cards and placing them to score points.

The rules of the game:

- Each player places tiles to build their own frosting shapes. Place colored dots to claim your building areas.

- When you close a shape, count one point for each tile in the shape. A shape that is not closed at the end of the game does not score any points.

- Add any bonus points labeled on your tiles to your score.

Example:

3+2=5 points

This frosting shape is worth 5 points.

Add 1 point per tile plus 2 bonus points.

Remember to mark your building area with a paper dot.

Yaaay!

Sugar Glaze Sugar Glaze Sugar Glaze Sugar Glaze
Sugar Glaze Sugar Glaze Sugar Glaze Sugar Glaze
Sugar Glaze Sugar Glaze Sugar Glaze Sugar Glaze
Sugar Glaze Sugar Glaze Sugar Glaze Sugar Glaze
Sugar Glaze Sugar Glaze Sugar Glaze Sugar Glaze
Sugar Glaze Sugar Glaze Sugar Glaze Sugar Glaze
Sugar Glaze Sugar Glaze Sugar Glaze Sugar Glaze
Sugar Glaze Sugar Glaze Sugar Glaze Sugar Glaze
Sugar Glaze Sugar Glaze Sugar Glaze Sugar Glaze
Sugar Glaze Sugar Glaze Sugar Glaze Sugar Glaze
Sugar Glaze Sugar Glaze Sugar Glaze Sugar Glaze
Sugar Glaze Sugar Glaze Sugar Glaze Sugar Glaze
Sugar Glaze Sugar Glaze Sugar Glaze Sugar Glaze
Sugar Glaze Sugar Glaze Sugar Glaze Sugar Glaze
Sugar Glaze Sugar Glaze Sugar Glaze Sugar Glaze
Sugar Glaze Sugar Glaze Sugar Glaze Sugar Glaze
Sugar Glaze Sugar Glaze Sugar Glaze Sugar Glaze
Sugar Glaze Sugar Glaze Sugar Glaze Sugar Glaze
Sugar Glaze Sugar Glaze Sugar Glaze Sugar Glaze
Sugar Glaze Sugar Glaze Sugar Glaze Sugar Glaze
Sugar Glaze Sugar Glaze Sugar Glaze Sugar Glaze
Sugar Glaze Sugar Glaze Sugar Glaze Sugar Glaze
Sugar Glaze Sugar Glaze Sugar Glaze Sugar Glaze
Sugar Glaze Sugar Glaze Sugar Glaze Sugar Glaze
Sugar Glaze Sugar Glaze Sugar Glaze Sugar Glaze
Sugar Glaze Sugar Glaze Sugar Glaze Sugar Glaze
Sugar Glaze Sugar Glaze Sugar Glaze Sugar Glaze

Sugar Glaze Sugar Glaze Sugar Glaze Sugar Glaze
Sugar Glaze Sugar Glaze Sugar Glaze Sugar Glaze
Sugar Glaze Sugar Glaze Sugar Glaze Sugar Glaze
Sugar Glaze Sugar Glaze Sugar Glaze Sugar Glaze
Sugar Glaze Sugar Glaze Sugar Glaze Sugar Glaze
Sugar Glaze Sugar Glaze Sugar Glaze Sugar Glaze
Sugar Glaze Sugar Glaze Sugar Glaze Sugar Glaze
Sugar Glaze Sugar Glaze Sugar Glaze Sugar Glaze
Sugar Glaze Sugar Glaze Sugar Glaze Sugar Glaze
Sugar Glaze Sugar Glaze Sugar Glaze Sugar Glaze
Sugar Glaze Sugar Glaze Sugar Glaze Sugar Glaze
Sugar Glaze Sugar Glaze Sugar Glaze Sugar Glaze
Sugar Glaze Sugar Glaze Sugar Glaze Sugar Glaze
Sugar Glaze Sugar Glaze Sugar Glaze Sugar Glaze
Sugar Glaze Sugar Glaze Sugar Glaze Sugar Glaze
Sugar Glaze Sugar Glaze Sugar Glaze Sugar Glaze
Sugar Glaze Sugar Glaze Sugar Glaze Sugar Glaze
Sugar Glaze Sugar Glaze Sugar Glaze Sugar Glaze
Sugar Glaze Sugar Glaze Sugar Glaze Sugar Glaze
Sugar Glaze Sugar Glaze Sugar Glaze Sugar Glaze
Sugar Glaze Sugar Glaze Sugar Glaze Sugar Glaze
Sugar Glaze Sugar Glaze Sugar Glaze Sugar Glaze
Sugar Glaze Sugar Glaze Sugar Glaze Sugar Glaze
Sugar Glaze Sugar Glaze Sugar Glaze Sugar Glaze
Sugar Glaze Sugar Glaze Sugar Glaze Sugar Glaze
Sugar Glaze Sugar Glaze Sugar Glaze Sugar Glaze
Sugar Glaze Sugar Glaze Sugar Glaze Sugar Glaze

Stuff your game pieces in here!

Fold on line.

Use glue stick here.

Cut, glue and fold to make the game piece envelope.

Use glue stick here.

Fold on line.

Cut on dotted line.

Explore
Discover
Excite

Forever   Bunt

Parents,

Play this STEM game with your child. Your budding scientist has been learning about how many things are made of smaller parts. It's math practice too!

Homework: How to play

1. Each player places tiles to build their own frosting shapes. Place a colored dot to claim an area to build off of.

2. When you close a shape, count one point for each tile in the shape and add any bonus points labeled on your tiles to your score.

Sugar Glaze!
The Game!

Sugar Glaze - Journal Entry

Depending on how you arrange the tiles to build your shapes, you can get different results. Play Sugar Glaze and you will see that no two games are the same.

Game 1 Score

You	Desk Partner

Game 2 Score

You	Desk Partner

Think, Pair, Share!

Why is it important to mix up the tiles in between games?

Many things are made of small pieces

As you saw in each activity, many complex things in this world are made of smaller parts. These smaller parts are then arranged or rearranged to make different larger things.

Explain the phenomenon:

What types of things can be made from smaller pieces?

_____

_____

_____

_____

_____

_____

_____

_____

Explain the
Phenomenon

Fun-Dixie Journal Entry

What did you like learning about or doing in this chapter?

_____

_____

_____

_____

_____

_____

_____

_____

_____

_____

_____

Royal
STEMTaught Post

When you read a great chapter in the STEMTaught Journal and do the fun activities inside, sometimes you just want to write about it!

Fold on line and tape or glue tab.

Royal
STEMTaught®
Post

Explore
Discover
Excite

To: _____

From: _____

Grade: _____

Teacher: _____

School: _____

Fold on line.

Fun-Dixie

Important!
Special Delivery

56